anythink

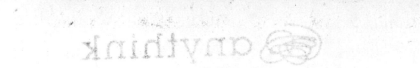

Peter's Bus Ride

A Book about Bus Safety

by Kerry Dinmont

Published by The Child's World®
1980 Lookout Drive • Mankato, MN 56003-1705
800-599-READ • www.childsworld.com

ISBN 9781503820357
LCCN 2016960948

Printed in the United States of America
PA02340

Today, Peter rides the bus.

How does he stay safe on his way to and from school?

Peter walks to the bus stop. He walks on the sidewalk.

ONE WAY

ONE WAY

Peter gets to his bus stop early. He waits three big steps behind the curb on the sidewalk.

The bus is here! Peter waits for it to stop. He will use the **handrail** as he walks on.

Peter goes right to his seat. He sits down. He does not stand up when the bus is moving.

The bus pulls up to Peter's school. Peter waits for it to stop before he gets up.

Peter has to cross the street. He waits. The driver **signals**. Now Peter can cross.

Peter walks five big steps in front of the bus. He never walks behind it.

How do you stay safe
on the bus?

Glossary

handrail (HAND-rayl) A handrail is a bar that people hang on to for support. Peter uses the handrail when he gets on the bus.

signals (SIG-nuls) Signals means using body motions to tell someone something. The driver signals when it is okay to cross the street.

Extended Learning Activities

1. Why is it important to walk in front of the bus instead of behind?

2. Why do you think school buses are yellow?

3. Have you ever ridden on a bus? Where did you wait for the bus? Did you stay sitting the whole ride?

To Learn More

Books

Garrett, Winston. *Let's Ride the School Bus!*
New York, NY: PowerKids Press, 2015.

Jennings, Rosemary. *Safe on the School Bus*.
New York, NY: PowerKids Press, 2017.

Web Sites

Visit our Web Site for links about bus safety:
childsworld.com/links

Note to Parents, Teachers, and Librarians: We routinely verify our Web links to make sure they are safe and active sites. So encourage your readers to check them out!

About the Author

Kerry Dinmont is a children's book author who enjoys art and nature. She lives in Montana with her two Norwegian elkhounds.